B̶

Practical Treatise
For Plain People

Also Available from LutheranLibrary.org

- *Gospel Truths: Presenting Christ and the Christian Life* by John Edwin Whitteker
- *New Testament Conversions* by George H. Gerberding
- *The Baptism of Children* by Emanuel Greenwald

About The Lutheran Library

The Lutheran Library is a non-profit publisher of good Christian books. All are available in a variety of formats for use by anyone for free or at very little cost. There are never any licensing fees.

We are Bible believing Christians who subscribe wholeheartedly to the Augsburg Confession as an accurate summary of Scripture, the chief article of which is Justification by Faith. Our purpose is to make available solid and encouraging material to strengthen believers in Christ.

Prayers are requested for the next generation, that the Lord will plant in them a love of the truth, such that the hard-learned lessons of the past will not be forgotten.

Please let others know of these books and this completely volunteer endeavor. May God bless you and keep you, help you, defend you, and lead you to know the depths of His kindness and love.

Baptism: A Practical Treatise For Plain People

By Rev. John Edwin Whitteker

Pastor of the Evangelical Lutheran Church of the Reformation, Rochester, NY

Utica, NY

THE YOUNG LUTHERAN COMPANY

© 1893 / 2019

(CC BY 4.0)

LutheranLibrary.org

Copyright Notice

This book was published 2019 by The Lutheran Library Publishing Ministry LutheranLibrary.org. Some (hopefully unobtrusive) updates to spelling, punctuation, and paragraph divisions have been made. Unabridged.

Originally published 1893 by the Young Lutheran Company, Utica, NY.

Cover image "Baptism of Pocahantas" by John Gadsby Chapman, 1840.

Image on imprint page is *Still Life With Bible* by Vincent Van Gogh.

This LutheranLibrary.org book is released under the Creative Commons Attribution 4.0 International (CC BY 4.0) license, which means you may freely use, share, copy, or translate it as long as you provide attribution to LutheranLibrary.org, and place on it no further restrictions.

The text and artwork within are believed to be in the U.S. public domain.

558 – v5
ISBN: 9781709090882 (paperback)

To
the Young Men and
Women of the Church of
the Reformation, brought to
Christ in Infancy by Baptism, and
instructed in the doctrines of the Divine
Word in Childhood and Youth, so that at
their Confirmation they were prepared to enter
intelligently upon the duties and
privileges that pertain to a consistent
Church Membership and a sound
Christian Life, this work is
most cordially inscribed
by their Pastor.

Table of Contents

Also Available from LutheranLibrary.org.............ii
About The Lutheran Library...........................iii
Copyright Notice......................................vi
Preface...xi
Preface by Lutheran Librarian........................xiii
Introductory Chapter. The Scope Of The Work...........1
Part 1. Who?..3
1. Untenable Objections Answered......................5
2. Scriptural Grounds For Infant Baptism..............9
3. Historical Grounds For Infant Baptism.............15
Part 2. How?...21
1. Baptize As A Heathen Word.........................23
2. Baptize As A Bible Word...........................27
3. New Testament Baptisms............................31
4. Scripture Argument For Sprinkling.................41
5. The Word Baptize As Used By Early Church Writers...49
Part 3. Why?...55
1. Why Be Baptized?..................................57
2. Benefits Of Baptism To Infants....................59
3. Scripture Argument For Baptismal Regeneration..65
4. How The Ancient Church Regarded Baptism..........69
Conclusion...73
How Can You Find Peace With God?.....................76

Benediction..77
More Than 100 Good Christian Books For You To Download And Enjoy..78

Preface.

THE ONLY APOLOGY that the author offers for the appearance of this little volume, is the time-honored principle that "self-preservation is the first law of nature," and that in common with his brethren in the faith, he is "set for the defense of the truth."

It is a notorious fact that our Lutheran people have been a constant prey to the proselyting methods of that body of believers known as Baptists. Realizing that some who waited on his ministrations were being infected with the poison peculiar to this insolent species of sectarianism, the author found it quite impracticable to go from house to house in order to administer the proper antidote, and the only alternative that seemed to meet the case was the issuance of a small volume such as this, embracing within as brief a compass as possible the entire subject, and adapted particularly to the wants of the rising generation. While its primary object is to keep the young people of his congregation in the faith of their fathers, it shall be a matter of rejoicing to him, if others, through its influence, are established in the teachings which its pages are designed to sustain.

In this work, the author lays but little claim to originality of thought. He has merely gathered together, largely from second sources, some of the leading Scriptural and historical facts bearing upon the subject; and while, in some respects it may justly be claimed that they are set in new relations and enforced by new arguments. still it is the same old truth confessed by the early Church. defended by all sound Protestantism and transmitted to our times as a precious legacy of the past.

The author, therefore, most heartily commends its attentive reading to the young people of his congregation and of the Church at large, with the hope that it may accomplish the purpose which has called it into being. And that the Great Head of the Church may use it for His own glory and the good of His children, is his most earnest prayer.

Rochester, N. Y., *Ash Wednesday*, 1893.

Preface by Lutheran Librarian

In republishing this book, we seek to introduce this author to a new generation of those seeking spiritual truth.

John Edwin Whitteker (1851-1925) attended Thiel College and the Lutheran Theological Seminary at Philadelphia, where he was appointed Latin Professor. He was ordained in 1877 and served pastorates in Rochester, NY, Easton, Lancaster, and Rochester, PA. Dr. Whitteker established at least 3 mission churches in his lifetime. He is the author of *Baptism: A Practical Treatise for Plain People* and *Gospel Truths*.

The Lutheran Library Publishing Ministry finds, restores and republishes good, readable books from Lutheran authors and those of other sound Christian traditions. All titles are available at little to no cost in proofread and freshly typeset editions. Many free e-books are available at our website LutheranLibrary.org. Please enjoy this book and let others know about this completely volunteer service to God's people. May the Lord bless you and bring you peace.

Introductory Chapter. The Scope Of The Work.

WHAT WE PROPOSE for you, dear reader, is a plain discussion on the subject of Baptism. We are led to this because of the persistent effort which is being made to undermine your faith and lead you to believe that you were baptized at the wrong time, and in the wrong way, and with a wrong notion as to the benefits which your baptism is designed to bring to you.

There are many cunning devices by which it is hoped to influence you to renounce your baptism and apply for it in another form and for a different purpose; and that you may be the better prepared to meet the arguments–or rather insolent assertions—which are being thrust upon you, and that you may become the better established in the faith of the Church, we ask you to give a careful study to this subject as presented in these pages.

The subject before us naturally divides itself under three heads:
1. Who is a Proper Subject for Baptism?
2. How is he to be Baptized?
3. Why is he to be Baptized?

To each of these questions we shall devote a distinct part of this little volume. Let us advance at once to their consideration in regular order.

Part 1. Who?

> "Go and make disciples of ALL NATIONS, baptizing them in the Name of the Father, and of the Son and of the Holy Ghost." St. Matt. 28:19.

> "Christ came to save all persons by Himself—all who are regenerated unto God [by Baptism], INFANTS and *little ones* and youths and elder persons."—Irenaeus.

Who, then, is a proper subject for Baptism? There being no question as to the propriety or validity of adult Baptism, the whole discussion here hinges upon the Baptism of Infants.

In approaching this subject, the first thing to be done is to answer unreasonable objections, produce the Scriptural authority for the Baptism of Infants, and show how history sustains the usage. To do this is a comparatively easy task. And if this can be done, not by wresting Scripture, but by putting upon it its own proper interpretation; not by bandying words, but by an unanswerable array of historical facts, the whole system of the Baptist sect falls to the ground, their excuse to exist as a distinct Church organization ceases, and upon them rests the responsibility of rending the Body of Christ, and of creating schism where there is no tenable ground for separation.

1. Untenable Objections Answered.

IN ORDER to show who is a proper subject for Baptism, let us begin by; taking a general view of the question, and along with it meet some of the so called arguments by which the effort is made to show that Baptism pertains only to adults.

1. As All Men Are Sinners, So All Stand In Need Of Salvation.

No one is regarded as a Christian unless he is a member of the Christian Church. No one is a member of the Christian Church until he is baptized. The Church has been established for all men, without any distinction whatever — it is for every human being.

To the question, Who stands in need of Baptism? there can be but one answer. Every one who stands in need of salvation — every human being, whether infant or adult. And so, without any limitation whatever, we claim that an infant, as well as an adult, is a proper subject for Baptism. To prove this is the purpose of these immediate pages.

2. Baptists Oppose This Claim

To this claim, however, the denomination known as Baptists directly oppose themselves. They say that there is no express command in the Word of God for Infant Baptism. They propose, at the outstart, to be very Scriptural. "To the Law and to the Testimony," they say. Their demand is, "Show us a positive command in the Bible to baptize infants and we will yield at once. And then they pause for a reply. We shall endeavor, in our humble way, to give them one.

But in so doing, we may be pardoned if we imitate the example of our blessed Master—answer one question by asking another. We challenge any and all who demand direct Scriptural authority for Infant Baptism to show us in the Word of God a positive command to observe the first day of the week as a day of rest, in the place of the seventh! The express command is, "Remember the Sabbath Day to keep it holy." Where is the express command to set aside this day and keep the one which the Christian Church so universally observes? There is none. Now, if Baptists wish to be consistent, they must either allow us to infer that Infant Baptism is an implied teaching of the New Testament, or they must unite with the "Seventh Day Baptists," in keeping the Jewish Sabbath. Until they hold "to the law and to the testimony," they must not try to force others to do so.

Not unlike this is the prevailing usage of admitting women as well as men to the Lord's Table. But it was not so in the beginning. When Christ instituted that sacred feast there were none with Him but His disciples—none but those twelve men. And there is not a single word of command uttered either by Christ or His Apostles that women should at any time be allowed to partake of the Holy Supper. The only authority that we have in this matter is the usage of the Church back through the centuries! But what right has any man or any set of men to demand direct Scriptural authority for admitting children to the Sacrament of Baptism, when they themselves, without a positive command, admit women to the Sacrament of the Lord's Supper? Why this straining at gnats in one instance, and swallowing camels in another? This attempt at pulling motes out of other people's eyes and considering not the beams that are in their own eyes?

And so, even if God's Word, in express terms, did not teach Infant, Baptism, the Baptists have no right to demand express teaching on the subject; for they violate that principle in other matters, finding only an implied teaching for the observance of the

Lord's Day in place of the Old Testament Sabbath, and allowing women to partake of the Lord's Supper when none but men were present at its institution. It is the boldest kind of presumption, on their part, to demand direct testimony in one case, and themselves be content with indirect testimony in another case!

3. *One Scripture Baptists Always Produce*

There is one passage of Scripture which the Baptists never fail to produce as an unanswerable argument against Infant Baptism: "He that believeth and is baptized shall be saved;" and then they triumphantly exclaim, "How dare you baptize an infant when you know it cannot believe?"

Now, it is a rule that what proves too much proves nothing at all. The misfortune with the Baptist argument here is that they do not quote the entire verse. They bring to the front what suits their purpose—stop right in the middle of the sentence, and by giving expression to a half-truth, become the advocates of the grossest error. The passage as it actually stands is: "He that believeth and is baptized shall be saved; but he that believeth not shall be damned." According to this, if a child must not be baptized because it cannot believe, it will be damned because it cannot believe; for "he that believeth not shall be damned!" If the Baptists say that the words referring to damnation do not apply to infants, we can, with equal propriety, claim that the words referring to belief do not apply to infants. If infants are not to be baptized because they do not believe, then they will certainly go to hell because they do not believe. What proves the one proves the other. We leave it with Baptist fathers and mothers to decide whether or not they will so interpret this passage of Scripture as to imply that their little ones, whose bodies they have laid away in the grave, are in that place of torment "where their worm dieth not and the fire is not quenched," or admit that these words cannot be used as an argument against Infant Baptism.

It would be interesting, right here. to take up the various passages of Scripture which are cited to show that infants should not be baptized; but as our chief aim is not to pursue fancies but to present facts, we shall turn, without further comment, to the Scriptural arguments in favor of Infant Baptism.

2. Scriptural Grounds For Infant Baptism.

THE SCRIPTURAL GROUNDS for Infant Baptism are both direct and implied; while the records of Baptism given in a Scripture make it a moral certainty that infants were baptized along with adults. The reasons for such an inference are so strong and positive that the burden of proof rests with those who debar infants from Baptism.

1. Infant Baptism Is Everywhere Implied In Scripture.

The very character of the Church, as set forth in the Word of God, furnishes a Scriptural warrant for it. There are two Covenants the Old and the New; but the Church is one. Under the Old Covenant, church membership pertained to children as well as adults. Under the New Covenant—that good thing of which the Old Covenant was but a shadow—church membership is surely as broad and all-embracing! The rite by which people were received into the Church in the days of the Old Covenant, was Circumcision. The rite by which people are received into the Church in this age of the New Covenant, is Baptism. Under the Old Covenant, infants were received into the Church when they were eight days old. And shall we not infer that it is proper to receive infants of any age, under the New, the broader Covenant? Surely this is not asking too much!

The only possible argument that can be urged against Infant Baptism is, that as there is no confession of faith, there is no assurance of faith. The same argument might have been urged against Circumcision. In the case of Abraham, as with every other person received into the Old Covenant under like circumstances, Circumcision was "a seal of the righteousness of the *faith* which he had being yet uncircumcised." In the case of the adult, therefore, faith was a condition preceding Circumcision and essential to Circumcision. And yet, right in direct contradiction to this principle, at the express command of God, "Abraham circumcised his son Isaac, *being eight days old!*" And so, in receiving infants into the Christian Church by the rite of Holy Baptism, we do no more violence to the institution of Baptism than Abraham did to the institution of Circumcision. At the direct command of God, the Jewish people received children into the Church by the rite of Circumcision, and had we no other authority than that here implied, we might, with equal consistency, receive children into the Christian Church by the rite of Baptism. It would be marvelously strange if there was a way of receiving children into the Church before the time of Christ, and none by which to receive them into the Church since His blessed advent. Strange, too, that while the rite by which grown people were received into the Jewish Church was used in the case of the child eight days old, the rite by which we are received into the Christian Church should be denied to our little ones!

Children became members of the Jewish Church by a positive law of God. When the Christian Church took its place, when and where was this law laid down: "Up to this time children have been received into the Church, but hereafter it shall not be so—from now on they are shut out!" Who for a moment can think that such was the purpose of Christ? of Him who said: "Suffer the little children to come unto me and forbid them not, for of such is the Kingdom of God!"

2. *God's Word Enjoins Infant Baptism*

But we go further and claim that God's Word, in express terms, enjoins Infant Baptism. Does not Christ plainly command: "Go and make disciples of all nations, baptizing them in the name of the Father, and of the Son, and of the Holy Ghost?" What other warrant do we need for the Baptism of children? What is a nation? Is it not made up of individual persons? And among the individual persons is there not included every human being from the very youngest to the very oldest? The command, therefore, to baptize all nations, is a command to baptize the youngest child as well as the oldest man. And for anyone to rise up and say that it means only the grown people, is to put an interpretation upon the words that is utterly false to the text!

Suppose the command had been, "Go and make disciples of all nations, circumcising them!" Would there have been any doubts as to the proper subjects for Circumcision? Suppose the proclamation be issued: "Go and take the census of the nation!" Does the agent stop and ask whether he is to count the babies too? How absurd, then, it is to say that when Christ commands His disciples to baptize all nations, He means only the big people! Suppose a man were to tell his servant, "Go and gather the sheep into the fold!" Out he goes, drives the sheep in, but leaves the lambs outside to perish in the storm! Will his master accept the apology that nothing had been said about the lambs? that he had only been told to shelter the sheep? Will he not meet his reply with a "thou fool!" And yet, the Baptist argument is just as silly and senseless as that of the shepherd who gathers the sheep into the fold, and leaves the lambs outside; because, forsooth, there is no absolute command to baptize infants, they are not mentioned by name! House the sheep, but expose the lambs! feed the nations, but starve the children! bring men and women into the Church by Baptism, but deny it to their little ones! Such is virtually the line of argument of those to whom Christ says in His displeasure, "Suffer the little children to come unto Me, and forbid them not, for of such is the kingdom of God." And by way of further rebuke and to show that they were susceptible to divine influence and capable of receiving God's grace, "He took them up in His arms, put His hands upon them, and blessed them!"

3. Examples of Infant Baptism Are Given In Scripture

Do we need any further confirmation that children are to be baptized? We have examples right in the word of God. In the 16th chapter of the Acts, we read that "Lydia was baptized and her household." In the same chapter we read that the jailer was baptized, "he and all his, straightway." Now, no one can, with any show of reason, deny that "he and all his" means himself and all his family ——wife and children—the entire household. Again, in the First Epistle to the Corinthians, Paul says that he "baptized the household of Stephanus." To say that there were no children in these homes is a piece of bold presumption. It would, indeed, be remarkable that these three families, together with the household of Cornelius and Crispus—making five families in all—should be baptized, and not a single child should be in one of them! And especially so, since the word "household" has direct reference to the children of the family, as is shown by the language of St. Paul to Timothy, when he says, "A bishop must be blameless, one that ruleth well his own *house*, having *his children* in subjection!"

Infant Baptism, therefore, is not a human invention, but has its authority of God Himself. This is implied in the fact that infants were received into the Old Covenant by the initiatory rite pertaining to that covenant; and we cannot but infer that they should be received into the New Covenant by its special initiatory rite, viz., Baptism.

Infant Baptism is distinctly enjoined by Christ—God manifest in the flesh—when He says: "Go and make disciples of all nations, baptizing them in the name of the Father, and of the Son, and of the Holy Ghost." And it is the shallowest kind of sophistry and a piece of supremest presumption to claim that the little children of the nations are not embraced in this command, because they are not mentioned by name. Neither are the women of the nation mentioned, nor the men, for that matter. It was not necessary to mention any in particular, for all were included,—men, women and children.

Infant Baptism was, beyond all question, a New Testament practice. Particular mention is made of five entire households that were baptized; and as house or household, according to New Testament usage, has special reference to the children of the family, it shows what wretched shifts the opponents of Infant Baptism will make and to what desperate straits they are reduced, when they deny that there were children in these families.

In view of all this, therefore, we unhesitatingly affirm that the Author of Infant Baptism is God Himself!

3. Historical Grounds For Infant Baptism.

IF GOD has actually set Infant Baptism in His Church, we must expect to find it there from the very first. History, of course, will not prove that it is of God; but if God ordained it and the Church practiced it, history will not be silent on the subject. Let us now see if history, in any way, sustains us in our affirmation. In other words, what are the historical grounds for Infant Baptism?

1. Justin Martyr

Justin Martyr, who was born before the death of St. John, in his "Apology for the Christians," says, "Many persons of both sexes, some sixty, some seventy years old, were made disciples to Christ from childhood." And let it be distinctly noted that the word here translated "Childhood" is the very one used in the New Testament, where we read that Jesus took "Infants" up in His arms. To the common reader, this may seem to say nothing about Baptism; but when we remember that "to be made a disciple" and "to be regenerated" were common terms with which to designate Baptism, it is very evident that what Justin Martyr means is that these aged men and women had been baptized in infancy. It is a fact beyond dispute, to quote the words of President Dwight, that "there never was any other mode of making disciples from infancy, except by Baptism." "And this usage," he adds, "grew out of the commission of Christ, 'Go and make disciples of all nations, baptizing them.'" There could be no discipleship without Baptism.

And so, those who were, according to Justin Martyr, "disciples from infancy," were most assuredly baptized in infancy. And the baptism of these people in infancy, takes us back at least twenty-five years before the death of St. John.

2. *Irenaeus*

Irenaeus was born within the last ten years of the first century. He was a pupil of Polycarp; and Polycarp was a pupil of St. John. Irenaeus says: "I can describe the spot on which Polycarp sat and expounded; his going in and coming out; the manner of his life; the figure of his body; the sermons he preached to the multitude; how he related to us his converse with John and the rest of those who had seen the Lord; how he mentioned their particular expressions, and what things he had heard from them of the Lord — of His miracles and of His doctrine." Surely, such a man is a competent witness!

What, then, is his testimony in this matter? He says, "Christ came to save all persons by Himself; all, I say, who are by Him regenerated unto God; infants and little ones and youths and elder persons." We must again remind you, dear reader, that Irenaeus, in common with all writers of the early Church, constantly used the word "regenerated," to mean "baptized." And so, this same writer in commenting on our Lord's commission to His Apostles to baptize, says: "When He gave His disciples the power of regenerating unto God, He said, 'Go and teach all nations, baptizing them.'" And he includes among those regenerated unto God by Baptism "INFANTS and *little ones*," as well as "youths and elder persons."

3. *Tertullian*

Tertullian was born a little later than Irenaeus. We may not be willing to accept all his teachings, but when it comes to the statement of a fact, he certainly is a competent witness. He believed that sin committed after Baptism could never be pardoned, and so he advised the delay of Baptism. It is for this reason that he says of the Baptism of Infants: "What need their innocent age make such haste to the forgiveness of sins?" By these very words, he acknowledges that the Baptism of Infants was a common practice. And while he speaks against it—to the great satisfaction, no doubt, of Baptists in general—he speaks against it, not as a *wrong* practice; but, because he believed that there was no pardon for sins committed after Baptism, as a *dangerous* practice. His testimony establishes beyond all question that the Baptism of infants was a common thing in his day.

4. Origen

Origen was born about 85 years after the death of St. John. As a writer, of whom it has been said that if the New Testament were lost, it could all be recovered again from his works, his testimony certainly should have some weight.

In his eighth homily on Leviticus, he says, "What is the reason why the Baptism of the Church, which is given for the remission of sins, is, by the usage of the Church, given to infants also?" He has a special purpose in asking this question. He is trying to establish the doctrine of original sin, and he brings forward the practice of Infant Baptism as a proof of it.

Again, in his fourteenth homily on St. Luke, he says: "Infants are baptized for the forgiveness of sins." Here, too, he aims to establish the doctrine of original sin. And so he says: "No one is free from pollution though he has lived but one day upon earth. And because by Baptism, natural pollution [that is, original sin] is taken away, therefore infants are baptized."

And once again, in his comment on Romans, he makes the significant declaration, which stands without challenge: "For this cause also it was that the Church received from the Apostles a tradition [the word is used in its better sense, meaning rather an order] to give Baptism to Infants." Is it, therefore, claiming too much when we say that the Apostles believed in and practiced

Infant Baptism? Would they give an order to do that in which they themselves did not believe, or which they themselves had not done?

5. Cyprian

Cyprian was born about the year of our Lord 200. At that time Infant Baptism was universally practiced. The question was then raised, not whether children should be baptized, but whether they might be baptized before they were eight days old. The matter was laid before the Church; Council that met at Carthage in the year 254. The convention was made up of sixty-six bishops, with Cyprian as their president. Their decision may be summarized in these words: "We all judged that the mercy and grace of God [by Baptism] is to be denied to no human being that is born. This was our opinion in the Council, that we ought not to hinder any person from Baptism and the grace of God, who is merciful and kind to us all. And this rule, as it holds for all, we think more especially to be observed in reference to infants, even to those newly born." Here are sixty-six bishops with Cyprian at their head, furnishing us the testimony that, in the middle of the third century, Infant Baptism was the common practice; and it was looked upon as so necessary, that if there was danger of a child not living till it was eight days old, it was baptized before that time.

6. Augustine

There are many other writers who speak expressly of the practice of Infant Baptism, but we shall close our testimony with a few quotations from Augustine, who lived during the fourth century.

In writing against the Pelagians, he says: "Since they grant that infants must be baptized—for they are not able to resist the authority of the Church, which was doubtless delivered by our Lord and His Apostles—they must consequently grant that they stand in need of the benefits of the Mediator."

In writing against the Donatists, touching the Baptism of Infants, he says: "Which, the whole body of the Church holds, as

3. Historical Grounds For Infant Baptism.

delivered to them in the case of little infants baptized—; and yet no Christian man will say they are baptized to no purpose."

In like manner he says, though even more specific: "The custom of our Mother Church in baptizing infants must not be disregarded nor accounted needless, nor believed to be anything else than an ordinance delivered to us from the Apostles."

And again, he makes the sweeping declaration that he "never met with any Christian, either of the General Church or of any of the sects, nor with any writer that owned the authority of the Scriptures, who taught any other doctrine than that infants are to be baptized for the remission of sin."

He goes even further and says: "The Whole Church practices Infant Baptism. It was not instituted by Councils, BUT WAS ALWAYS IN USE."

Here we close our testimony on this point. And in so doing, we feel constrained to affirm with Pelagius, who lived in the fourth century: "I have never heard of any, not even the most impious heretics, who denied Baptism to infants!" Adding this, however, so as to bring the declaration up to date, Baptists, only, excepted!

Therefore, to the question, Who is a proper subject for Baptism? we reply in the spirit of the Church in all generations, and in perfect harmony with the New Testament practice, so far as that practice is made known to us, and in obedience to. the command of Christ. " INFANTS, and *little ones*, and youths and elder persons!"

Part 2. How?

> "Then will I SPRINKLE clean water upon you. and ye shall be clean." Ezekiel 36:25.

> "POUR on the head water thrice, in the Name of the Father and Son and Holy Ghost." —Teaching of the Twelve Apostles.

We come now to our second question, "How is Baptism to be administered?" In the light of everything; that bears upon this subject, the question is not merely what mode or modes, may be allowed; but what mode is the most consistent—the most in keeping with everything that is associated with our Baptism.

To decide this, we must have a correct conception of the word "Baptize." The Baptists, who arrogate to themselves the word with all its broadness, and narrow it down to "all their utter littleness, assert that it has but a single meaning, TO IMMERSE—always means that—never means anything else! We claim that, in its strict meaning, it is not bound to any particular mode—it rarely deals specifically with mode. The mere going into the water, or even under the water, does not constitute a baptism. If a boy jumps into a river, he is not baptized, he is simply immersed, especially if he is drowned; for immersion, in the strict sense of the word, puts one down below the surface of the water, but it makes no provision for taking him out. In short, to immerse, according to the primary meaning of the Word, means to drown. When the devils went into the swine, the whole herd ran violently down a steep place into the sea and were—immersed— were plunged under and stayed under!

This instance is not cited as an argument against Immersion as it is now understood, but simply to show that it might be well for the Baptists to mend their own language, before they attempt to tinker at that of the Bible.

The question directly before us is, How are we to determine the meaning of the word "Baptize?" Evidently by its use in literature—Classical. Biblical and Christian, at the same time adducing such Scriptural argument and Scriptural analogy as may aid us in determining its limitations from a Christian point of View.

Let us now look in that direction and see just what this word " Baptize" reveals to us.

1. Baptize As A Heathen Word.

IN ORDER to understand the exact meaning of the word "Baptize," we must go back to original sources. Let us see, then, what use the ancient heathen writers made of it. In so doing. it would be desirable to introduce the Greek; but that would not serve the purpose of those for whom this work is intended, and so we must reduce everything to plain English. We shall also confine ourselves to a few of the many examples at hand, for in the mouth of two or three witnesses every word shall be established.

1. The Original Word

Let us begin by going a step back of the original word from which "Baptize" is derived, and see what it means. There is a comic poem, entitled "The Battle of the Frogs and the Mice." This battle, we are told, took place on the borders of a lake and "the lake was baptized with blood;" or, as one of our English poets puts it:

> "A purple stream of blood
> Distains the surface of the silver flood."

Imagine Homer saying that the lake was immersed in blood— dipped in blood! It would be rather a difficult task—a veritable labor of Hercules— to take up a lake and plunge it into the blood of frogs and mice! The lake was baptized, i.e. colored with blood, tinged with blood—the blood trickling down into it and coloring its waters, In all seriousness, if one can be serious when dealing with such undiluted nonsense as pervades the Baptist system, the theology that makes baptize, in every instance, mean immerse, if run off in rhyme, would make a better comic poem even than "The Battle of the Frogs and the Mice."

2. The Meaning of "Baptize"

But now to the exact meaning of the word "Baptize" itself. The Greeks likened success to a bottle riding on the surface of the water. The ancient bottle was made of the skin of an animal, and when blown up, like a bladder or football, it would ride upon the waves without sinking or even suffering the water to pass over it. The prophecy concerning Athens was: "Thou mayest be baptized, O bottle, but it is not allowed to thee to go under." Here is a sort of baptism in which the subject, a skin bottle, or bladder, could not go under the water, or be immersed, but was tossed upon the wave, and only the spray could be dashed upon it. The bottle was baptized—sprinkled by the spray, but not immersed.

3. Aristotle's Example

Aristotle tells us of a "land uninhabited; whose coast was full of sea weeds." At ebb tide, it was not baptized; but at full tide the waters dashed over it. Here is a "baptism" of low lands, and a baptism by pouring. The land was not picked up and plunged into the sea—that would have been immersion; but when the tide came in, the sea poured a small part of its contents over the land, and so it was baptized—baptized by the pouring of water upon it. The water was applied to the land. not the land to, the water. It was a clear case of pouring.

4. Aristophanes

Aristophanes, in speaking of the Platonic banquet, says: "I am one of those *baptized* yesterday"—*drenched with wine*, is his real meaning. He was not plunged into a tank of wine and left there to pickle!—not *immersed* in it.

And so we read in another place that Alexander was *baptized with wine*. Wine was not the thing into which he was plunged so that the stuff came clear over his head; it was the thing with which he was drenched. It was a baptism with wine by pouring, not into wine by immersion.

5. Ships Sinking

Among the favorite examples which the Baptists delight in quoting to sustain immersion, is that great array of instances in which the word baptize is used to represent ships sinking to the bottom of the sea. We are willing to accept every such recorded instance as thoroughly genuine. These seamen and their ships were immersed in the one and only original sense—they went to the bottom of the sea, *and they stayed there!* And so, if the Baptists really insist upon these examples as a proof that there must be a going under the water in order to be baptized; we can, with equal right, insist that there must be a staying under the water in order to be baptized. Imagine Christ saying: "He that believeth and goeth to the bottom of the sea and stayeth there shall be saved!" or Peter demanding of the Jews, "Repent and be drowned every one of you for the remission of your sins!" That would be a severely literal way for a man to lose his life in order to save it. And yet, if the exact meaning of the word "baptize" is to be determined by these cases of shipwreck, consistency demands that we put just such absurd speech into the mouth of Christ and His Apostle.

From the foregoing examples, which might be multiplied, it is clear that the word "Baptize" has a variety of meanings other than immerse. And when Baptists claim that it means immerse and nothing but immerse in Classic Greek, they claim that which the instances just cited prove to be without foundation.

2. Baptize As A Bible Word.

LET US NOW SEE what Jewish custom reveals concerning Baptism. We are not to suppose for a moment, that Baptism was a thing sprung upon the people by John, the forerunner of Christ. There were baptisms in the Jewish, as well as in the Christian Church, each, of course, having its own significance. Just as the heathen use of the word had no religious significance, so the Jewish use of the word had no Christian significance.

In speaking of the Jewish ritual, St. Paul says that it "stood only in meats and drinks and divers Baptisms." What some of these "baptisms" are, the Apostle clearly tells us.

1. Blood and Ashes

He says (Heb. 9:13, 14.) "For if the blood of bulls and of goats and the ashes of a heifer sprinkling the unclean, sanctifieth to the purifying of the flesh, how much more shall the blood of Christ... purge your conscience." Surely the Jews were not dipped into blood and ashes. On the other hand, it is distinctly stated that they were sprinkled; and this sprinkling St. Paul counts among the "divers baptisms."

2. Blood of Calves and Goats

St. Paul goes on to say (v. 19:) "For when Moses had spoken every precept to all the people, according to the law, he took the blood of calves and of goats, with water, and scarlet wool and hyssop, and sprinkled both the book and all the people." And when the Law of Moses with its "divers baptisms" was superseded by the Gospel of Christ, then came the fulfillment of that prophecy, "So shall He sprinkle many nations." If Isaiah had only said, "So shall he dip many nations," every Baptist heart would leap for very joy. But Isaiah said nothing of the kind. He was a prophet, and told the truth!

##3. Hands

What some of these "divers baptisms" were, we also learn from St. Mark. He says (8:34): "For the Pharisees and all the Jews, except they wash their hands oft, eat not, holding the tradition of the Elders. And when, they come from the market, except they wash, they eat not. And many other things there be which they have received to hold, as the washing of cups and pots, brazen vessels, and of tables."

Let it be noted here that the clause "except they wash," literally translated would read, "except they have baptized themselves"; and "washing," literally translated would read, "Baptisms." It need scarcely be mentioned that to "wash" refers to the custom of washing the hands. It is a cunning device to claim that they dipped themselves in water. There is nothing in this connection to warrant such a conclusion. On the other hand, the Jews have kept the custom, to this very day, of washing their hands—baptizing themselves—before eating. And no less cunning—and contemptible as it is cunning—is the effort to make it appear that this washing, this baptism of the hands, was a dipping of the hands into the water, and therefore an immersion. The remarkable fact is that the Jews never dipped their hands into the vessel containing the water, but the water was poured out over their hands—a practice which prevails in the East to the present day.

4. Wine

At the house in Cana, where the marriage feast was held, there were six waterpots of stone, after the manner of the purifying of the Jews. These held two or three firkins apiece. Just how much that is, we do not know; but the highest estimate fixes the quantity at a little more than half a barrel. These, mark you, were for the purifying, the washing, the Baptisms of the wedding guests. Just how the entire company were going to immerse themselves in these stone jars, we leave to the fertile brain of some Baptist to explain. We confess our utter inability to do so!

5. *Tables*

Among the things that the Jews baptized, St. Mark mentions tables. The marginal reading in our English Bible calls them "beds," better rendered, perhaps, by the word "couches." Can anyone in his senses suppose, for a moment, that these couches were immersed? This is a passage which has given the Baptists a great deal of trouble; but finally one of them, with a greater inventive genius then the rest, somehow got the brilliant idea into his head that it was possible that these couches were so constructed as to be taken to pieces and then immersed—because, go under the water they must! For real fresh originality, this transcends anything that we have ever read outside of the famous fabrications of Baron Munchhausen.

It would fill a book to discuss the purifications of the Jews as they are referred to in the New Testament. The foregoing are ample to show that at least some of these purifications, these washings, these Baptisms, were either by sprinkling or pouring—not by immersion. And so we again have proof positive that the word "Baptize," does not by any means always, or even ordinarily, mean "Immerse."

3. New Testament Baptisms.

We are now ready to turn to the New Testament and look into the individual cases of Baptism that are recorded there. A very fertile field lies before us, full of interesting facts; beginning, as it does, with the Baptism of John—which we must bear in mind was not Christian Baptism—and taking in the whole range of early Church practice, so far as that practice is revealed to us in the writings of the Apostles.

It may safely be assumed, by this time. that the word "Baptize" does not always mean immerse; that it really sometimes means to pour or sprinkle!, unless, perchance, we have written in vain. In fact, we run no great risk in assuming that the very common New Testament use of the word is to sprinkle or pour, and we need not be at all surprised to find that the persons whose Baptism is mentioned in Scripture were baptized by pouring or sprinkling. Let us see just how this matter stands.

1. How Did John Baptize?

The Scripture testimony is that John did baptize in the wilderness. It was the wilderness of Judea—a desert place—a place where, after leaving the Jordan, one can travel for miles and not find a drop of water. Josephus, the Jewish historian, says of it: "The whole plain is destitute of water, except the Jordan." No wonder, then, that John baptized in the Jordan! As "the voice of one crying in the widerness," he must perform the work of his ministry in the wilderness, and the only place where this could be done with comfort to himself and convenience to the people, was along the banks of the Jordan.

But, you may ask, what about that passage of Scripture where it is said that "John was baptizing in Aenon, because there was much water there!" Well, how "much water" was there really there? Was there a great rolling river? or deep pools? or broad lakes? There is not very much known about Aenon, but the universal judgment is, to use the description of another, that "Aenon are little springs gushing out, whose waters are soon absorbed by the sand." Why, then, did John go to Aenon? We must bear in mind that there "went out to him Jerusalem and all Judea, and all the region round about Jordan." Such a mass of people would need much water, not for immersion, as the Baptists claim; but for drinking. The "much water" of Aenon, or literally, its "many waters"— i.e. its many little springs, whose streams "are soon absorbed by the sand," would make it preferable to any of the desert places along the Jordan. It is very evident, then, that the "much water" of Aenon was not used by John for the purpose of immersion; on the other hand, immersion in this, "much water" was an utter impossibility!

In all that is said of John's Baptism, there is nothing which specifies absolutely the exact mode—all that can be done in any case is to infer how it was performed. We have, however, one ground of inference which carries with it the weight of direct testimony. Since "divers baptisms" of the Jews, which were for the "purifying of the flesh," were performed, as we have already shown, by pouring or sprinkling; it is surely reasonable to infer that when John baptized unto repentance, he performed the act according to the very common usage of pouring or sprinkling. Surely a baptism unto repentance would not require any more water than a baptism for a purifying of the flesh! Besides, that John baptized in the Jordan, no more proves that he plunged the people into its waters than that he baptized in the wilderness proves that he thrust them into the sand!

2. *How was it in the case of Jesus?*

He came to John to be baptized of him. And when John forbade Him, Jesus said: "Suffer it to be so now, for thus it becometh us to fulfill all righteousness." It need scarcely be said that "to fulfill all righteousness," means to fulfill the law——'not the traditional law—Jesus did not pretend to keep that. He even sat down to eat without washing His hands—a sin in the eyes of the Pharisees as great as homicide.

But why was Jesus baptized at all! His Baptism could not have been unto repentance; for He had nothing of which to repent. It could not have been for the remission of sins; for He had no sins to be forgiven, and as for the sins of others, He was crucified—not baptized—for their remission! What possible reason, then, could there have been for his Baptism? And in receiving it at the hands of John, what law did he fulfill? We find a clue to this in the declaration that He was not baptized till He was thirty years old.

Christ came to be our Prophet, Priest and King. In each of these offices there was a law to fulfill. How did he fulfill all righteousness in entering upon the duties of His priestly office?

(1.) No One Could Officiate As A Priest Until He Was Thirty Years Old.

oThe law was: "From thirty years and upwards until fifty years they shall enter into the tabernacle for the service of the ministry." When Christ was thirty years old He began His ministry. He obeyed the law to the very letter.

(2.) No One Could Officiate As A Priest Until He Was Duly Consecrated To Its Ministry.

The law required a twofold Baptism in consecration—a Baptism of water and a Baptism of oil. The law touching the former was: "Take the Levite [for the priesthood] from among the children of

Israel and cleanse them. And thus shalt thou do unto them to cleanse them, sprinkle water of purifying upon them... that they may execute the service of the Lord." Now, what righteousness, what part of the law was fulfilled in the Baptism of Jesus, if not the one that demanded that He should be sprinkled with water upon entering His ministry? There is absolutely nothing else to account for it!

(3.) In Addition To The Baptism Or Sprinkling With Water, There Was The Baptism Or Anointing With Oil.

The law read: "Then shalt thou take the anointing oil and pour it upon his head and anoint him." Jesus certainly was anointed; for the very name "Christ" means the "Anointed One." But His anointing was not common; for His was not a common priesthood —He was anointed with the Holy Ghost. This is the plain declaration of the Word of God; for Peter tells Cornelius "How God anointed Jesus of Nazareth with the Holy Ghost."

The Baptism of Jesus, therefore, was a complete Baptism—the earthly and the heavenly being combined in it. The water was sprinkled upon him, and the Holy Ghost was poured out upon Him. Both descended from above—the water from the hand of John, the Holy Ghost from heaven in the form of a dove. There was no t more a dipping into the water than there was a dipping into the dove; but as was the mode of the heavenly, so was the mode of the earthly—both came on the head from above. There is not a single circumstance to show that Jesus was immersed, but everything points unmistakably to sprinkling as the mode of His Baptism.

3. *The Ethiopian Eunuch*

How was it with the Baptism of the Ethiopian Eunuch? The simple record is: "And they went down both into the water, both

Philip and the Eunuch, and he baptized him." (Acts 8:33.) This looks very much like immersion, you say; for they went down into the water. This word "into" does not prove anything. And for two reasons:

(1.) The Greek Word Often Means "To"

The Greek word to which it corresponds very commonly means "to"—a striking illustration of which is furnished us by St. John, (20:4): "One came to the sepulchre, yet he went not in—the word here rendered "to" being the very same one which is rendered "into" where it says. "They went into the water." So you see the English word "into" proves nothing.

(2.) The Going Into Was Not The Baptism

But suppose they did go into the water. That did not constitute the Baptism; for Philip went in as well as the Eunuch, but only the Eunuch was baptized. In that case, there must have been some special act of Baptism after they were in the water. What was it? We have no hesitancy in saying that this baptismal act was one of sprinkling or pouring. And this also for two reasons:

The first is the very nature of the country. The command to Philip was "Arise and go toward the south, unto the way that goeth down from Jerusalem unto Gaza, which is desert." There was not "much water" there! The road runs through a long stretch of desert country. Here and there is to be found a little rill of water, bordered with green; otherwise the country is desert. And here it was, that Philip joined himself to the Eunuch's chariot. For once, at least, we are away from deep water!

The second reason lies in that which was engaging the mind of the Eunuch, and which led to his Baptism. He was reading the Bible—the prophecy of Isaiah. And the particular point that he did not understand; was the fifty-third chapter and the seventh and eighth verses. His question with respect to it was: "'Of' whom speaketh the prophet this? Of himself or some other man?" Then

Philip began to teach him—began, we are told, "at the beginning." The beginning of this prophecy concerning Christ is with the fifty-second chapter and the thirteenth verse, "Behold, my servant shall deal prudently," etc. The fifteenth verse reads: "So shall he sprinkle many nations!" The conversation, as the sequel shows, turns upon Baptism. The hearer is impressed with its importance. If this man of whom the prophet speaks shall sprinkle many nations, and the day of fulfillment is now at hand, should he not be among those whom He shall sprinkle? And then, we can imagine him looking up, and, seeing one of those little streams which burst out here and there in the desert, his exclamation of mingled joy and surprise is, "See, here is water! What doth hinder me to be baptized?" And so, alighting from the chariot, they both went down to the water and Philip baptized him. How? There is no deep-flowing river in that desert place—nothing but little rills, and not very many at that! Besides, the man had just read, "He shall He sprinkle many nations!" And would he then say, "What doth hinder me to be dipped?" Would not his thought be, if Christ shall sprinkle many nations why should I not be sprinkled too?

Laying aside every other consideration which points to sprinkling, the mere fact that the place was a desert and that the Scripture that Philip was explaining to him contained the passage, "So shall he sprinkle many nations"—this should of itself be sufficient to convince any man who is not stubbornly set to sustain a sectarian notion, that the Eunuch was baptized by sprinkling.

4. The Baptism of Paul

The Baptism of Paul does not furnish the least scrap of evidence in favor of Immersion. There was no "going down into the river" in his case, or "coming up out of the water," which the Baptists roll as a sweet morsel under their tongues. Take your Bible and read the account as given in the 9th Chapter of the Acts. See how explicitly everything is stated—into what apparently unimportant details the writer goes. Paul rose from the earth; Opened his eyes but saw no man; was led by the hand and brought into Damascus; and for three days he was without sight and did neither eat nor drink. Note, in the next place. the command given to Ananias: "Arise and go into the street which is called Straight and inquire in the house of Judas for one called Saul of Tarsus, for behold he prayeth." See how Ananias carries out his instructions: He went his way and entered into the house and putting his hand on him said, Brother Saul, the Lord, even Jesus that appeared unto thee in the way as thou camest, hath sent me that thou mightest receive thy sight and be filled with the Holy Ghost." And then what followed? "Immediately there fell from his eyes as it had been scales, and he received sight forthwith, and arose and was baptized; and when he had received meat he was strengthened."

Now, dear reader, picture to yourself this scene. VVhere did it all occur? In a house! You can not possibly paint a river in this picture, unless you have a crazy imagination. From the moment that Ananias entered the door, till Paul received food and was strengthened, everything was enacted within the walls of that house! Just think of it—for three days, Paul did neither eat nor drink. Weak and blind, there he lay, helpless creature that he was! And when the scales fell from his eyes, he arose—stood up—and was baptized. There is nothing to show that he took a single step, but the implication rather is that he stood still—and was baptized. Then they gave him something to eat and he was strengthened. It takes a very strong imagination and a wonderful amount of ingenuity to represent Paul tottering along with Ananias till they come to the nearest river, see him plunged beneath its surging waters, brought out again, and then taken back to the house of Judas;——and all the while, there is not one word to show that he took a single step away from that couch. The only fact that we have is, Paul "stood up and was baptized." And the only possible way for such a Baptism to be performed is by sprinkling or pouring.

5. *Cornelius and His Family*

Take the case of Cornelius and his family and friends (Acts 10:44—48). The record is that while Peter was speaking, "The Holy Ghost fell on all them that heard the word." There were some Jews present, and they were astonished "because that on the Gentiles also was poured out the gift of the Holy" Ghost." And Peter said, "Can any man forbid water that these should not be baptized?"

But when Peter went up to Jerusalem he was taken to task for having anything to do with these Gentiles. And so, he rehearsed the whole matter, concluding with the words, "And as I began to speak, the Holy Ghost fell on them as on us at the beginning. Then remembered I the word of the Lord, how He said, John indeed baptized with water, but ye shall be baptized with the Holy Ghost." He reasoned thus: These people have received the Holy Ghost; can any man forbid water? They have received the heavenly which is greater; can any man, forbid the earthly, which is less? And if the Holy Ghost fell on them as He did on Peter himself and the other Apostles in the beginning, shall not the water fall on them also? Their Baptism by water thus being the Seal of their Baptism by the Holy Ghost! Surely the mode of the less shall not contradict the mode of the greater—the earthly shall not contradict the heavenly!

There can be but one verdict with respect to the Baptism of Cornelius and those with him—they were baptized by pouring or sprinkling. It is utterly impossible to read immersion into the case. There is not a single attendant circumstance to suggest it.

6. *The Jailer and His Family*

One more example and we are done with this point—the Baptism of the jailer and his family (Acts 16:19—34). Read the account through and then ask yourself, What evidence is there that there was a tank in the prison, or a river running through it, or that Paul led the jailer and his family out to some river or water tank and there immersed them? There is none. Any such inference or supposition is but the freak of a diseased mind! The plain fact is, that Paul would not leave the prison till those who had unjustly thrust him in there would themselves come and take him out. And as to a tank in the prison—really the suggestion is too weak to be treated with serious consideration.

Now, in all these instances, there is not the least proof that anyone of these Baptisms was by immersion, but there is clear evidence that in the majority of cases, immersion was an utter impossibility. On the other hand, there is evidence in every case that the mode employed was that of sprinkling or pouring; and in some cases it was the only possible mode that, under the circumstances, could be employed. The records of the New Testament, therefore, plainly indicate—not immersion, but sprinkling or pouring as the Scriptural mode of Baptism.

4. Scripture Argument For Sprinkling.

LET US NOW ADVANCE to the direct Scriptural argument for Sprinkling. This might have been urged in each of the cases just cited; but these were considered purely in the light of attending circumstances, and not judged from any direct teaching on the subject. To look into that direct teaching is the task now before us.

1. Baptism With Water and The Holy Ghost Are Closely Linked.

Beginning with the Acts of the Apostles, where the Christian Church first stands out distinctly as an institution of God, we find, as we might expect, that Baptism with water and Baptism with the Holy Ghost are very closely related to one another. As far as the Church is concerned, God has joined them together, and no man may put them asunder.

Already in Acts 1:5, we have a declaration on Baptism from the lips of Christ Himself: "For John truly baptized with water, but ye shall be baptized with the Holy Ghost not many days hence." In this short passage the word "Baptized" occurs twice: "Baptized with water;" "Baptized with the Holy Ghost." In each instance it expresses an act; and the mode of that act, if there is any consistency in human speech, exactly corresponds in the one case to that of the other. If, therefore, to baptize with water, means to dip into the water; then, by a plain and unfailing law of language, to baptize with the Holy Ghost means to dip into the Holy Ghost. If it means to dip or immerse in the one case, it means to dip or immerse in the other.

Let us now turn to the Scriptures and see just how this matter stands. 'A few days after Jesus said, "John truly baptized with water, but ye shall be baptized with the Holy Ghost not many days hence," came the day of Pentecost—that day of glorious fulfillment when the Holy Ghost was poured out upon men. It was their Baptism with the Holy Ghost—the very Baptism promised by Christ! When the crowd sneered and said, "These men are full of new Wine!" Peter replied, "These are not drunken as ye suppose... But this is that which was spoken by the prophet Joel, And it shall come to pass in the last days, saith God, I will pour out of my Spirit upon all flesh, ...and on my servants, and on my hand maidens, I will pour out in those days of my Spirit." And toward the close of that powerful argument, Peter said, "Wherefore, being by the right hand of God exalted, and having received of the Father the promise of the Holy Ghost, He hath *shed forth* this which ye now see and hear." Who that has any conception of language, or any regard for God's Truth, or any fear of God's Judgment, would dare to read Immersion into these words!

As in this instance, so in the whole range of prophecy, the gift or Baptism of the Spirit is always spoken of as a pouring out, a shedding forth, or a sprinkling, i.e. if any reference is made to mode. For example:

> Isaiah 44:3, "I will pour my Spirit upon thy seed;"
>
> Isaiah 52:15, "So shall He sprinkle many nations;"
>
> Ezekiel 36:25, "Then will I sprinkle clean water upon you, and ye shall be clean."

As in prophecy, so in fulfillment. When men were baptized with the Holy Ghost, the Holy Ghost fell on them. And it is for this very reason that we sincerely believe that, when they were baptized with water, the, water fell on them. We no more believe that they fell into the Holy Ghost, than that they fell into the water! The case, therefore, resolves itself into this: If Baptism with water means a dipping" into the water, then Baptism with the Holy Ghost means a dipping into the Holy Ghost. But if our Baptism with the Holy Ghost means a pouring out, a shedding forth, a sprinkling, then, if language means anything, or there is any such thing as analogy, the one consistent mode for our Baptism with water is the pouring out, the shedding forth, the sprinkling of water upon us.

It is a most wretched subterfuge to which some resort when they say that in the case of these disciples the room was filled with the Holy Ghost, and; therefore the Holy Ghost immersed them, — an inference as coarse and crude as it is fictitious and unfair. The Scripture does not say that the Holy Ghost filled the room, —it was the sound that "filled all the house where they were sitting."

This first record of Baptism in the Christian Church—an immediate Baptism of the Holy Ghost—was unmistakably a Baptism by sprinkling, for "cloven tongues like as of fire" "sat upon each" one of the assembled disciples; and no amount of prostitution of words or perversion of facts can set this truth aside. And yet, Baptists tell you that the word "baptize" always means "immerse,"——cannot possibly mean anything else!

2. "We Are Buried With Christ By Baptism"

There is one passage of Scripture that the advocates of immersion always have at their tongue's end, "We are buried with Christ by Baptism;" and, of course, what else can that mean than going under the water! The simple fact is, it has nothing whatever to do with mode. Turn to your Bible again, dear reader, and examine what St. Paul says on this matter. It is recorded in Rom. 6:3—6. Here, you see, is mentioned the whole round of Christ's redeeming work—His crucifixion, death, burial and resurrection. What is there in any mode of Baptism to correspond with the crucifixion of Christ? Nothing; absolutely nothing! What, to correspond with His death? Again nothing; absolutely nothing! Why, then, shall a resemblance be sought out between immersion, on the one hand, and the burial and resurrection of Christ on the other, and nothing be said of His crucifixion and death? And the more so, since the specific thing upon which the likeness rests is His death? Why this ominous silence on these two points, and this posting in a conspicuous place of the other two points, unless, forsooth, the merest reference to the former would break down a pet theory—a theory which must be sustained even if Scripture is silenced in Order to do it! The crucifixion and death were effected upon the Cross; Immersion could have nothing in common with them. But the words "burial" and "resurrection," according to modern ideas, seem to fit so exactly to being buried under the water and raised up from it again, that many people see nothing but the very prototype of immersion in them, and it is really a pity to spoil so sweet a vagary. But the truth must be told though the heavens fall!

And now for the truth of the matter. St. Paul says: "Know ye not that so many of us as were baptized into Jesus Christ, were baptized into His death?" Now, if it is literally true that believers are to be buried under water in Baptism, then, by the laws of language, it is literally true that they are to be put to death in Baptism. The principal idea here is the dying. 'It is the one thing insisted upon—the one thing upon which the entire meaning Of the chapter turns. It is here distinctly stated that believers are buried with Him by Baptism "into death;" that they are planted together "in the likeness of His death;" that they are crucified with Him; that they are baptized into "His death." The central thought is His death and the mode of that death; and if the resemblance lies in the mode, then find it, if you can, in Christ's dying on the Cross and a man going down under the water! The fact is, there is no reference here whatever to the mode of Baptism: the Apostle is dealing entirely with its blessed effects.

More than this, there is no mode of Baptism, be it sprinkling, pouring, or immersion, that has anything in common with these words. Take it in the case of the burial. What is there in common between plunging a living man under water, and carrying a dead man into a cave? We must not look for the resemblance in the way in which we bury our dead. The body of Jesus was not lowered into a grave: the ground was not poured over it. It was carried into a room of living rock and stretched upon a rocky bed, with nothing to touch it but the ledge on which it lay. The two acts have nothing in common. They are as unlike as water and rock themselves.

Again, take it in the case of the resurrection. Imagine, if you can, the seal of that tomb bursting, and an angel, with countenance like lightning and raiment white as snow, rolling the stone away;—imagine Jesus folding the bands of linen, laying them carefully aside, and then walking forth from the open door, on past those keepers who had become as dead men. Can you picture to yourself anything quite as majestic or quite as sublime? Now look upon that other scene—a human being dipped into the water and then lifted out—poor drowning, dripping thing, strangling and struggling for breath—the sorriest sight that eye could well behold! Find, if you can, dear reader, the least resemblance between that poor gasping creature just pulled out of the water and the Conqueror of death and hell walking forth in triumph from the open door of the sepulchre, and we shall forthwith yield every point which these pages aim to establish.

It would be interesting to take up this whole matter, as stated here by St. Paul. and range beside it the silly stuff which is linked with it in order to sustain the doctrine of immersion; but the whole thing resolves itself into the grotesquely absurd and would drag down the grand theme of the Gospel, "Christ on the Cross, the only King," and make it most painfully ridiculous. The entire subject is quite too sacred for that. What little ridicule has unavoidably crept in, can be defended, only on the principle that We must "answer a fool according to his folly." And now we desist from pursuing immersionists' imaginings on this particular passage any further, on the ground that a man's folly may become so utterly foolish that one must "answer not a fool according to his folly."

3. 1 Cor. 10:1-2

Another specific reference, bearing upon the mode of Baptism, is, made by St. Paul in 1 Cor., 10:1; 2. Here the Apostle declares that all the Israelites were "baptized unto Moses in the cloud and in the sea." Surely there was enough water here to immerse the Israelites —men, women and children. But they were not immersed. That distinguished honor was reserved for Pharaoh and his host! The fact is, the children of Israel, in their Baptism. walked on dry ground. There was no immersion at all, in their case. But if we may be so reckless as to set up a declaration of fact (Ps. 77:15, 16, 17, 20) against sectarian fancy, it was a clear case of sprinkling. The Psalmist says:

> "Thou hast with Thine arm redeemed Thy people, the sons of Jacob and Joseph. The waters saw thee, O God, the waters saw Thee; they were afraid; the depths also were troubled. The clouds found out water... Thou leddest Thy people like a flock by the hand of Moses and Aaron."

Now this accords exactly with what St. Paul says:

> "All our fathers were under the cloud... And were all baptized in the cloud and in the sea."

How? As they walked on dry ground through the bed of the sea, they were baptized in the sea—the sea was the place in which their Baptism occurred—the dry bed of the sea. They were baptized in the cloud—How? The cloud, according to the Psalmist, poured out water. It was this that constituted their Baptism, and it was a baptism by sprinkling—the water pouring out from the clouds and falling in drops, just as we see it in any summer shower.

It is the sheerest nonsense for anyone in serious mood to call this a dry dip, as some have done. It is strange what straws drowning men will grasp at. A dry dip! One might as well 'talk' of wet sunshine!

4. 1 Peter 3:20-21

The last passage of Scripture to which we shall refer in this connection is 1 Peter 3:20, 21, where we read that there were "eight souls saved by water, the like figure whereunto even baptism doth also now save us." How any man of ordinary brains and everyday common sense can find any resemblance between immersion and Noah and his family riding safely above the waters of the great flood, we cannot understand, unless we are to regard it as another of those "dry dips." But such refinements are altogether too subtle for us. There was, indeed, a great immersion on that memorable occasion; but Noah and his family, by the good providence of God, mercifully escaped it. They stayed above water; although the water may have fallen in copious drops upon them.

The fact is, there are only two well authenticated cases of Immersion in the whole range of Bible History—that of the unrepenting world, immersed by the flood, when Noah and his family were saved from immersion; and that of Pharaoh and his host, who were immersed in the sea; while the children) of Israel passed over on dry ground.

In View of all this we are solemnly constrained to add a new petition to the Litany: "From all forms of Immersion, Good Lord, deliver us!"

5. The Word Baptize As Used By Early Church Writers.

As a fitting conclusion to this Second Part, it may be interesting to see how the word "baptize" is used by the early Church writers, where reference is made to the mode. And, by the way, since these men all spoke Greek, we may take it for granted that they had about as good an idea of what the word which we render "baptize" meant, as our contemporaries do, who with the aid of Grammar and Dictionary can scarcely struggle through a Greek sentence!

1. Early Church Writers

Clemens of Alexandria, in speaking of a backslider who had been reclaimed, says that he was baptized a second time with tears.

Tertullian recognizes sprinkling as a proper mode of Baptism when he says: "Who will accommodate you, a man so little to be trusted, with one sprinkling of water?"

Origen in his comment on 1 Kings 18:33, represents the wood on the altar over which Elijah gave commandment that water should be poured, as having been baptized.

Lactantius says that Christ received Baptism that he might save the Gentiles by Baptism, i.e., by the distilling of the purifying dew.

Gregory Nazianzen says: "I know of a fourth Baptism, that of a martyrdom and blood;and I know of a fifth, that of tears."

Many of the Church Fathers, in particular Cyprian and Jerome, interpret the prophecy of Ezekiel 36:25, "I will sprinkle clean water upon you," as referring to Baptism.

Justin Martyr speaks of deliverance from evil passions as a Baptism. Ambrose calls the sprinkling of the blood of the passover lamb in Egypt a Baptism. Athanasius enumerates several kinds of Baptism, one of which is that of tears. Cyril says that the sprinkling of the ashes of the heifer on the unclean is a Baptism. Anastasius, among other things, mentions affliction as a Baptism. Chrysostom refers to the fact that Christ calls his crucifixion and death a Baptism. Nilus calls tears of penitence aBaptism.

But why multiply examples? Surely the foregoing are sufficient to satisfy any reasonable soul. In all these instances, two things are clear beyond question. The first is that in not a single case can the word " dipping" or "immersion" be substituted for that of Baptism. The second is that the only mode, if any, indicated by these examples is that of sprinkling or pouring, or some kindred expression. Immersion is ruled clear out!

2. *The Sick And Feeble*

It is a well-known fact of history that the sick and feeble were baptized; by pouring or sprinkling. Novatian and Constantine were so baptized. Jerome and Augustine speak of a thrice dipping, not of the whole body, but only of the head, as a mode of Baptism common in the Ancient Church. One of the martyrs, a little while before he suffered, baptized one of his executioners with a pitcher of water.

A peculiar instance is recorded of a Jew who was taken sick while traveling with some Christians and desired Baptism at their hands. It was in a desert place and having no water, they sprinkled him three times with sand, in spite of the fact that they had a most glorious opportunity of most literally burying him by baptism! The man recovered; his case was reported; and the official decision was that he was baptized, if only he have water poured on him again.

3. "The Teaching of the Twelve Apostles"

Perhaps nothing has so startled the Baptist world as the discovery a few years ago, of the "Teaching of the Twelve Apostles"—a work which is . recognized as perhaps the most ancient document of the Christian Church outside of New Testament writings. The seventh section reads as follows:

> "And touching Baptism, thus baptize: Having first declared all these things, baptize in the name of the Father, and of the Son, and of the Holy Ghost, in living water. But if thou have not living water, baptize in other water; and if thou canst not in cold, then in warm. But if thou have neither, pour on the head water thrice in the name of Father and Son and Holy Ghost."

Here is an explicit statement coming right from Apostolic days, that immersion is not necessary to a valid Baptism. Whether running or stagnant, cold or warm, it made no difference—a little water poured on the head three times, in the name of the Father and of the Son, and of the Holy Ghost, was all that was needed! And here is a point worth noting. The Baptists used to immerse, as a rule, in living water; but they rarely do so any more. They used to immerse in cold water—the colder the better; but now they make it comfortably warm. One step more—may we dare to hope as much? and they will reach the mode of pouring water on the head, and then at last the Church will have ONE BAPTISM!

To conclude this part: We do not say that there is no historical ground for immersion—simply that there is no Scriptural ground for it. It has a history, and that history reaches back to a very early age of the Church; But that of itself! does not prove anything in its favor. There is not an abomination in the Romish Church, that has not an historical basis of some kind. That a thing has been done once is, in itself, a very poor authority for doing it again. If such were the case, every vice would become a virtue, and every crime a

Christian grace. A fundamental doctrine of the Church must not only have its witness in history, but also its warrant from the Divine Word. And here is just where the Baptist system fails. While there is historical ground for immersion as a mode of Baptism, there is absolutely no historical ground for it as the only mode of Baptism. And when you bring it to the test of Scripture, there is nothing whatever to sustain it, general or particular, direct or implied—nothing but the coarse inference of a crude age.

Besides, what is so disastrous to the Baptist theory, is the fact that the very same ancient authority which determines immersion as a mode of Baptism, determines also that the devil is to be driven out by exorcism, that salt shall be put on the subject's tongue, that his eyes and ears and mouth shall be anointed with spittle and—tell it not in Gath—that this subject, whether man, woman, or child—it mattered not—should be first stripped of all clothing and then thrust under the water. The very same ancient authority which establishes immersion, establishes all such folly and impropriety!

Let others do as they please in this matter, but we beg to be excused from indulging in any of these disgusting crudities and downright indecencies which link themselves with so-called "historical" immersion, and of which, in our age and clime, immersion itself is no small part. There is not a mind of delicate mold but revolts from the whole thing—immersion included—and all the refinements of modern methods have failed to strip it of its revolting nature.

The crudities of a simple age may be winked at, but to try to revive them and tack them on to our modern civilization is a piece of coarse-grained empiricism. We do not say that civilization, in any sense, outstrips Christianity; on the contrary, Christianity leads civilization; but, it is nevertheless true, that the Church in her methods rises but little above the civilization of the age. And as the civilizing forces of Christianity are exercised upon the methods of men, the operations of the Church receive the benefits of its refining touches, and are elevated in proportion to its influence. Civilization has set nothing aside that has been established as an essential element of Christianity, but it tones down the crudities

5. The Word Baptize As Used By Early Church Writers.

and eliminates the vulgarities that an untutored age may have attached to the operations of the Church. Immersion is not a primary principle of Christianity. All that can possibly be claimed for it is that it was a primitive practice, but as such it has no more claim upon us than the salt and spittle and naked dipping of the primitive age to which these things are peculiar, and with whose death it also should have died. It has no warrant from the Word of God, and it should have no place in that civilization which is the direct product of the Word of God

Part 3. Why?

> "Repent and be baptized every one of you FOR THE REMISSION OF YOUR SINS." – Acts 2:38.

> "Infants are to be baptized FOR THE REMISSION OF SINS." – Augustine

WE NOW COME to the third and last part of the general subject of Baptism: Why are we to be Baptized? There must be some substantial reason for the institution and use of Baptism, otherwise it would be a piece of supreme nonsense to contend for it, and especially for any particular mode of it. If it is not set as one of the essential elements of the Christian religion, it would be far better to cast it aside altogether, and not divide the Church on a thing which, in itself, is only an empty form. It is an act of gross wickedness for any body of believers to cut loose from the Church unless it is for a principle that is essential to the very life of the Church.

As we cannot conceive of the Christian Church without Baptism, it must by God's ordination be fundamental to the very existence of the Church. And the rank assigned it by the Church at the beginning, and which it still holds among all so-called orthodox denominations, shows that the Church Universal has a due sense of its fundamental character. Let us, in the following chapters, see where the Scriptures rank it, what reasonable grounds there are for it, what Scriptural arguments can be drawn in favor of it, and what benefits the early Church attached to it.

1. Why Be Baptized?

Why, then, be baptized at all? Jesus says: "He that believeth and is baptized shall be saved." Peter declares: "Repent and be baptized every one of you for the remission of your sins." Ananias, that devout man, says to Saul: "Arise, and be baptized and wash away thy sins, calling on the name of the Lord." St. Paul's testimony is, "Christ also loved the Church and gave Himself for it, that He might sanctify and cleanse it with the washing of water by the Word."

1. *Baptism Worketh The Forgiveness of Sins*

These Are But A Few Of The Many Passages Of Scripture Which Set Forth, The Benefits Of Baptism. It is not essential, however, for the declaration of the principle to quote them all. Enough is here given to substantiate what Luther long ago said:

> "Baptism [by which he means the Holy Spirit through Baptism] worketh the forgiveness of sins, delivers from death and the devil, and Confers everlasting salvation on all who believe as the word and promise of God declare."

Or, to quote the language of a certain professor in a certain Baptist Theological Seminary, when, in summing up the a various passages of Scripture which set forth the benefits of Baptism, he says:

> "These are, I believe, the only passages in the New Testament which declare the use of Baptism, and the only passages which declare the use of Baptism say with up-and-down directness that Baptism *regenerates, remits sin and saves.*"

Here, for once we will agree with a Baptist—not because he is a Baptist, but because for once his testimony on this subject agrees with the Word of God. It is only when he departs from the plain testimony of that Word and the consensus of the Christian Church in all ages, that we take issue with him.

2. Baptism Regenerates, Remits Sin, and Saves

It cannot, therefore, be disputed on Scriptural grounds and Christians who are not warped by dogmatic definitions or tainted with the New Theology, will not, as a rule, dispute that Baptism regenerates, remits sin, and saves. The common Christian consciousness is often nearer the truth, than profound systems of faith. Tell a wayfaring Christian that Christ says: "Except a man be born of water and of the Spirit, he cannot enter into the Kingdom of God," and he will at once acknowledge that Baptism is necessary to salvation. Tell him that St. Paul says: "According to His mercy He saved us by the washing of regeneration and renewing of the Holy Ghost," and he will be ready to confess that Baptism regenerates, remits sin, and saves. It is one of those beautiful instances in which "God hath chosen the foolish things of the world to confound the wise."

2. Benefits Of Baptism To Infants.

There are, then, individual Christians in-all branches of Christ's Church—even the most crooked—who are ready to acknowledge the saving effects of Baptism. The Scriptural statements are so positive and unequivocal. that their strong Christian sense compels assent to them. But many of them will limit all such saving effects to adults—they cannot see how an infant can be made partaker of them.

There are so many plausible reasons given why infants cannot be benefited by Baptism, that we deem it proper to meet those who advance them—not only by arraying the positive declarations of Scripture against them, and entrenching ourselves behind doctrinal statements; but also by stepping out as it were, into the open field and meeting them right on their own ground.

1. Infants Cannot Believe

The universal cry is, Infants cannot believe, and so they cannot partake of the blessed benefits of Baptism. How do we know that they cannot believe? Samuel was dedicated to God, even before he was born. John was filled with the Holy Ghost from his very birth. Christ speaks of those little ones that believe in Him. Timothy knew the Scripture from a child. Whence is any man's faith? It is the gift of God, wrought by the Holy Spirit, through means of God's appointment. And if God works faith, who will limit His power and say, "Thus far and no farther shalt Thou go?" If God works faith in adults by means suited to their estate as adults, can

He not work faith in infants by means suited to the estate of infants?

How soon do we have any evidence of natural faith in a little child? As soon as it is born, it nestles to its mother's bosom. If God has put natural faith in it—call it instinct or whatever you please—along with its natural generation; can He not put spiritual faith in it by means of spiritual regeneration? Is He not equally great as the God of grace as He is as the God of nature? We know that the spiritual birth of John the Baptist was co-incident with, if it did not, perhaps, antedate his natural birth; and whoever is least in the Kingdom of God is greater then was he? It is folly for us to limit the power of God by our poor senses, or set bounds to the operations of grace by our weak judgments.

Again, how soon does a little child give evidence of Christian faith? As soon as it can lisp its first word. Does the mere ability of the child to speak its faith prove that there was no faith there until it was able to express it? As well argue that the first steps a child takes prove that it has no legs till it is able to walk! The ability of the child to walk shows that the animal powers were there in embryo; the ability of the child to give expression to Christian faith shows that spiritual powers were there in embryo. But since by nature we are dead in trespasses and in sins, spiritual life is a thing implanted in us by the Holy Ghost through means of God's appointment. And as Baptism is the washing of regeneration and renewing of the Holy Ghost, it is the means of God's appointment for giving the child that spiritual life which, with its first words, manifests itself in Christian faith.

2. *No One Can Enter Heaven Without Renewal*

"That which is born of the flesh is flesh;" and "except a man"—a human being, man, woman or child— "be born again, he cannot see the kingdom of God." No one, not even a child, therefore, can enter heaven without the renewal of its nature. Those dying in infancy must be regenerated, and regenerated by the power of the Holy Spirit. Cannot the Holy Spirit exercise His regenerating power on a living infant through His own appointed means as well as on a dying infant without any established means? The region of grace throughout, is the region of the miraculous. Acknowledge the power to be of God, and the work to be God's work, and the miracle of grace is no more wonderful in the case of an infant than it is in the case of an adult. To say that God cannot regenerate a child by means of Baptism is to say that He cannot regenerate it without Baptism, and you force the inference that every child dying in infancy makes its bed in hell! But admit that God works regeneration in a dying child, and you must admit that He can no less in the case of a living child; and the means which He has set for this and through which He declares that He effects this, is Baptism. It is the only way which God has ordained for reaching a child through the agency of the Church; and therefore, the Church has in all ages baptized infants for the remission of their sins and the bestowal of God's grace.

Every godly mother prays for her child, however young it may be. She prays, not merely for its animal nature, but especially for its spiritual nature. She prays God that He may make it His child—not when it is twelve or fifteen years old; but that it may be His from its very birth. She prays that it may have every spiritual benefit and blessing right from its very birth. Why does she pray thus, unless deep down in her heart is the conviction that God can bestow spiritual benefit and blessing upon her child, and that He will actually confer them in answer to her prayer! And if God will bless spiritually a little babe in answer to its mother's prayer of faith, can He not and will He not bless it spiritually, by a Sacrament of His own appointment? Especially since we know that there is no way instituted in the Church by which a child can be savingly reached. except by means of a Sacramental Act! The simple fact is this: Infant Baptism and Infant Regeneration, by means of Baptism, call for no higher exercise of Christian faith on the part of parents than do their prayers, or the prayers of the Church, offered up in behalf of little children. The very same objections that are raised against baptizing infants for their regeneration can be raised against praying for infants that they may be spiritually blessed. And until Baptist ministers quit praying for spiritual blessing upon little children, they have no right to interpose objections to the Baptism of Children for their spiritual good.

3. The Baptists Pride Themselves In Being Very Apostolic In Their Mode Of Baptism.

Without acknowledging their claim, we may still admit that they are decidedly primitive in some other respects. They even antedate Apostolic times and get right back to those very days when the disciples rebuked those who brought little children to Jesus. And Jesus says to them what He said in His displeasure to His well-meaning but sadly mistaken disciples: "Suffer the little children to come unto Me and forbid them not, for of such is the Kingdom of God." And then He showed them by word and act, not only that a little child is capable of receiving God's grace, but also that we must humble ourselves to their estate if we would become partakers of that grace. Hence He declared:

> "Verily I say unto you, whosoever shall not receive the Kingdom of God as a little child, he shall not enter therein!"

And then "He took them up in His arms, put His hands upon them and blessed them." And what he did to those little children immediately, without any visible means, He now does to our little children mediately, through visible means—The Institution of Holy Baptism!

Let us inquire a little further into this act of Jesus. What did He do to these infants? And what was the effect of that which He did? He put His hands upon them and blessed them! There was an act and 'a result of that act—a sacred ceremony with its own peculiar blessing. Who would dare to say that Christ performed this act just to please those fond mothers? that it was a sham performance on His part, whose only aim and end was flattery? If, then, these children actually received a blessing, was it temporal or spiritual, present or future? Christ is here speaking of the kingdom of heaven, and the conditions on which we enter it. And the only inference that can be drawn from the whole incident is that when He put His hands on those little children and blessed them, they then and there received some actual, positive, spiritual blessing. And if those children were capable of spiritual blessing directly at the hand of" Jesus, who will dare affirm that they can receive no spiritual blessing indirectly from Him, through a Sacrament of His own appointment, especially in view of the fact that the disciples were, sent forth to carry on the very work which Christ had instituted and the method declared was, "Go and make disciples of all nations, baptizing them in the name of the Father, and of the Son, and of the Holy Ghost!"

We have no more right to refuse Baptism to infants, because we cannot understand how spiritual blessing is associated with that divinely appointed institution, than the disciples had to rebuke mothers for bringing their little ones to Jesus, because they could not understand how spiritual blessing could come to them from being brought to the Saviour. But just as Jesus took them up in His arms and blessed them—yea, and they were blessed—so the Church takes up the little children and administers to them the Sacrament of Baptism, assured that Whatever blessing God's Word attaches to Baptism is guaranteed to these little ones by the operations of God's Spirit. Let us not be faithless but believing.

3. Scripture Argument For Baptismal Regeneration.

So far, we have given the plain testimony of Scripture—the mere Scriptural fact—that Baptism regenerates, remits sin and saves, together with a few inferences to be drawn from it. There are many passages whose proper interpretation leads us to the same conclusion. Let us now take one or two of these and see what arguments may be drawn from them.

1. Effects, Not Mode

In discussing the mode of Baptism, we showed that the Apostle refers not to its mode, but to its effects, when he says:

> "Know ye not that so many of us as were baptized into Jesus Christ, were baptized into His death; therefore we are buried with Him by Baptism into death; that like as Christ was raised up from the dead by the glory of the Father, even so we also should walk in newness of life."

The argument briefly stated here is, we are dead with Christ; for "so many of us as were baptized into Jesus Christ, were baptized into His death." Being dead with Christ, we should no more live a sinful life than a dead body lives a natural life. We are not only dead, we are buried by Baptism into death—dead and buried. Just as the burial is the proof of the natural death; so also, Baptism, to every child of God, is the witness of his death unto sin; with this difference, however, that Baptism is not only the sign of the death and burial, but also the means for effecting the death and burial of' "our old man." "Dead unto sin!" "Alive unto Christ!"—such, then, is the specific teaching of this passage of Scripture, and the means ordained of God for effecting this death and implanting this life is distinctly declared to be Baptism.

Let us now enter into a brief analysis of these words of St. Paul and see how beautifully they bring out, in regular order, the blessed effects of Baptism.

1. "Baptized into Christ, Jesus."

Our baptism brings us into Christ Jesus—into His body, which is the Church. It makes us a part of that living organism of which He is the Head.

2. "Baptized into Christ, we are" baptized into His death."

Just as Christ died for sin, so are we to die unto sin. But before we can die unto sin, Christ's death must be made our own—we must be baptized into His death. Being baptized into His death, our old man is crucified with Him and the body of sin is destroyed.

3. But Christ not only died. He also rose again.

And just as He. "was raised Up from the dead by the glory of the Father, even so we also should walk in newness of life." This is the purpose for which Baptism was ordained of God and the effect which it was designed to produce. It clearly indicates that Baptism is more than an initiatory rite by which we are brought into covenant relation with God—that it is more than a means by which there is an individual imputation of the death of Christ. It institutes a new relation. It is an engrafting into the body of Christ, so that the life which flows from Him, flows out into us as living branches. In the clear and concise words of Dr. Greenwald:

3. Scripture Argument For Baptismal Regeneration.

> "With Christ, the baptized Christian is crucified and his sins are taken away, since Christ bore them in His own body; with Christ on the Cross he dies, and the body of sin is destroyed; with Christ he is buried, and lays away and puts off the body of death; with Christ he rises to a new spiritual life in God; with Christ he walks on earth in righteousness and true holiness; with Christ he will live in heaven in glory forever."

And all this the Apostle here declares to be the blessed effect of Baptism.

2. *"The Washing of Regeneration"*

Again, take those other words of St. Paul:

> "Not by works of righteousness which we have done, but accOrding to His mercy He saved us by the washing of regeneration and renewing of the Holy Ghost."

It is impossible to misunderstand language such as this. The reference plainly is to Baptism and to the effects of Baptism. What, then, is the exact teaching of these words?

1. The first is purely negative.

It tells us by what we are not saved— "not by Works of righteousness which we have done." Salvation is not of us.

2. The second teaching is positive.

> "According to his mercy He saved us."

Salvation, as here classed, points to the merciful kindness of God. "It is of the Lord's mercies that we are not consumed because His compassions fail not." And His merciful compassion finds expression in the redeeming work of Christ—the Work that He has done for us.

3. There must not only be a saving work for us —there must also be a saving work in us.

That work is called regeneration and renewal. It is a work accomplished by the Holy Spirit, and the means which He employs in its accomplishment is Baptism; for "according to His, mercy He saved us by the washing of regeneration and renewing of the HOLY GHOST."

The comment of Dr. Alford on these words is worthy of reproduction:

> "Here is no figure: the words are literal. Baptism is taken in all its completeness—the outward visible sign, accompanied by the inward spiritual grace. And as thus complete, it not only represents, but is the new birth; so that it is not the mere outward act or fact of Baptism to which we attach such high and glorious epithets, but that complete Baptism of water and the Holy Ghost, whereof the first cleansing by water is indeed the ordinary sign and seal, but whereof the glorious indwelling Spirit of God is the only efficient cause and continuous agent."

In short, it is not what we do in Baptism, but what God does through Baptism, that gives it its efficacy, the water of Baptism being the earthly element by which the Holy Spirit communicates the heavenly grace.

And such, throughout, is the plain and unmistakable testimony of God's Word, wherever the least reference is made to the blessed effects of Baptism,—it is the divinely appointed means through which God by His Spirit "regenerates, remits sin and saves." Let us earnestly contend for the faith once delivered to the saints.

4. How The Ancient Church Regarded Baptism.

Since Baptism from the very first took so important a rank in the Christian Church, we may expect to find some reason assigned for the prominence given to it. And in this we are not disappointed, for the history of Baptism abounds in statements which show what benefits the early Church invariably associated with it. We shall be very brief in our citations; and in making them, it will be necessary to quote, in part, much of the historic evidence adduced to sustain Infant Baptism, for in all these the benefits of Baptism are clearly indicated.

1. Justin Martyr

The words of Justin Martyr are not without much weight, showing, at least by implication, the benefits of Baptism when he says:

> "Many persons of both sexes, some sixty, some seventy years old, were made disciples to Christ from childhood."

The outward mode of becoming disciples of Christ in childhood is quite generally acknowledged to be Baptism. It is the only way in which a little child can become a disciple of Christ. These people, then, were Christians, and their Christian life—i.e., their new life in Christ—is dated from their baptism. It was to them, as it is in the case of every Infant Baptism, the washing of regeneration and renewing of the Holy Ghost. it was their New Birth, developing into that fulness of Christian life, which went on from strength to strength till the end of their days.

2. *Irenaeus*

Irenaeus says: "Christ came to save all persons by Himself—all, I say, who by Him are regenerated unto God," And to show what he means by being regenerated unto God, he adds: "When He gave His disciples the power of regenerating unto God, He said unto them, 'Go and teach all nations, baptizing them." By a very common figure of speech he puts the effect for the cause, and in so doing he sets forth what he regards as the one great benefit of Baptism better than he could have done by the clearest line of argument. He states the effect rather than explains the process; for who can explain a mystery of God! It is very evident, then, that Irenaeus taught Baptismal Regeneration.

3. *Tertullian*

Tertullian taught that Baptism was the means of washing away sins; for, speaking of Infant Baptism, he said: "What need their innocent age make such haste to the forgiveness of sins?" He thought that sins committed after Baptism could never be pardoned, and so he would delay Baptism, so that one might have the full benefit of its blessed effects.

4. *Origen*

Origen also speaks of being baptized for the forgiveness of sins, when he says that "the Baptism of the Church is given for the remission of sins." With his thorough knowledge of the New Testament, he could not well teach otherwise; for it is one of the plainest declarations of Scripture that we are to be baptized for the remission of our sins.

5. Augustine

Augustine sets it down as an accepted truth "that infants are to be baptized for the remission of sins."

6. Pelagius

Pelagius asserts that Baptism is administered "for the remission of sins."

It was therefore the judgment of the early Christian Church, even with some of the most heretical, that Baptism is a means of grace. So positive was this conviction and so universal was its acceptance, that Augustine, that man of profound Christian scholarship and broad general knowledge, affirms that he "never met with any Christian either of the general Church, or of any of the sects, nor with any writer that owned the authority of the Scriptures, who taught any other doctrine than that infants are to be BAPTIZED FOR THE REMISSION OF SINS." It is not for us to take up the Nicodemus cry: "How can these things be?"

It is for us in common with God's people of all time, who have been biased, neither by human tradition, on the one hand, nor by human reason, on the other, to accept the great Scriptural fact that "Baptism doth also now save us;" that as many "as have been baptized into Christ, have put on Christ;" that Christ's means of sanctifying and cleansing the Church is "with the washing of water by the word;" and that "except a man be born of water and of the Spirit, he cannot enter into the Kingdom of God."

More than this—The same kind of argument that will explain away Baptismal Regeneration, will also explain away every other truth of the Bible. It is a significant fact that where the Church adheres to the plain Bible teaching on the Sacraments, her whole system of doctrine is comparatively pure; but let her once depart from these, and she plunges into all kinds of treacherous quicksands, and nothing short of a miracle of grace can extricate her. Next to the doctrine of justification by faith, the doctrine of the Sacraments is the barometer which marks the Church's fidelity or infidelity to the pure principles of the Gospel.

It is also a significant fact, that the same faith and knowledge that gave forth the great fundamental doctrines of the Church, also gave forth the teaching that we are baptized for the remission of our sins; and that, in our Baptism, where all the Scriptural conditions are met, we have the remission of sins. And we know that where there is remission of sins, there also are life and salvation.

Let us not be ashamed of the testimony of the Gospel that Baptism is "The washing of regeneration and renewing of the Holy Ghost." Let us confess in the language of the Nicene Creed: "I acknowledge one Baptism for the remission of sin." Let us accept the verdict of the Church universal, that we are " regenerated unto God by Baptism." Let us give our most hearty assent to that article in the Augsburg Confession which reads:

> Of Baptism they teach that it is necessary to salvation, and that by Baptism the grace of God is offered, and that children are to be baptized, who, by Baptism, being offered to God, are received into God's favor."

And let us remember that all the promises of God are YEA and AMEN, leave to Him their perfect fulfillment, and trust Him for His grace.

Conclusion.

In view of the positive Scripture testimony, and the strong historical evidence gathered together in the preceding pages, these three points are settled beyond all dispute:

1. INFANTS are proper subjects for Baptism, as well as adults.
2. SPRINKLING or POURING is the most consistent mode for the administration of Baptism.
3. THE REMISSION OF SINS is the great purpose and the unfailing end of Baptism, where all the Scriptural conditions are met.

With these truths before us, founded on Scripture and witnessed to by the Church in all ages, it becomes us, who have been baptized in infancy, to look upon our Baptism as thoroughly valid and availing for all time. It is God's covenant with us as well as our covenant with God, and His covenant stands fast forever. What remains for us is to be faithful to our baptismal vows, and wherein we fail, or fall short of their fulfillment, to return to them again, strive to live in accordance with them, and seek God's grace that we may be kept faithful in their observance unto the end.

The one thing which we should bind upon our foreheads to mark our "Holiness Unto The Lord," and the one thing which we should study to understand and in view of which we should live, is the covenant made with us in our Baptism by God, and renewed by us in our confirmation before men. It is the point at which God meets us with His grace, and we meet God by coming under the regenerating and renewing power of the Holy Ghost. And if, at any time, through the allurements of the world, the weakness of the flesh, or the wiles of the devil, we break our covenant with God, we know that God's covenant with us stands sure. We cannot undo with our iniquity what He has done in equity and in truth; and the satisfying assurance of this will save us from despair and lead us to turn to God with repentant hearts and seek His grace anew.

Baptism is not a ceremonial act in which we bring sacrifice to God; it is a sacramental act in which God brings life and salvation to us. To nourish this new life and to sustain it in its growth, He has instituted the preaching of the Word and the Sacrament of the Altar; and the faithful use of these means will enable us to go on from strength to strength, till God shall perfect that which He has begun in us, and we shall, by that other mighty working of God, be transferred from this kingdom of grace, which we entered as infants at our Baptism, to that kingdom of glory, where we shall have attained that perfection of life of which our Baptism was the germ, and where we shall enjoy that perfection of bliss which was assured us in our Baptism by a covenant-keeping God.

Then let us not be carried about with every wind of doctrine, by the sleight of men and cunning craftiness, whereby they lie in wait to deceive. Let us rather accept the great truths of Scripture, stand fast in the faith of the Gospel and true to the principles of our Church, and with her children everywhere lift up our voices in the words of that noble hymn:

> 1 Father, Son, and Holy Spirit,
>   I'm baptized in Thy dear Name;
> In the seed Thou dost inherit,
>   With the people Thou dost claim, I am reckoned;
>   And for me the Saviour came.
>
> 2 Thou receivest me, O Father,
>   As a child and heir of Thine;
> Jesus, Thou who diedst, yea, rather
>   Ever livest, Thou art mine. Thou,.O Spirit,
>   Art my Guide, my light divine.

3 I have pledged, and would not falter,
   Truth, obedience, love to Thee;
I have vows upon Thine altar,
   Ever Thine alone to be; And for ever,
   Sin and all its lusts to flee.

4 Gracious God, all Thou hast spoken
   In this covenant shall take place;
But if I, alas! have broken
   These my vows, hide not Thy face; And from falling
   O restore me by Thy grace!

5 Lord, to Thee I now surrender
   All I have, and all I am;
Make my heart more true and tender,
   Glorify in me Thy Name; Let obedience
   To Thy will be all my aim.

6 Help me in this high endeavor,
   Father, Son, and Holy Ghost!
Bind my heart to Thee for ever,
   Till I join the heavenly host. Living, dying,
   Let me make in Thee my boast.

How Can You Find Peace With God?

The most important thing to grasp is that no one is made right with God by the good things he or she might do. Justification is by faith only, and that faith resting on what Jesus Christ did. It is by believing and trusting in His one-time *substitutionary* death for your sins.

Read your Bible steadily. God works His power in human beings through His Word. Where the Word is, God the Holy Spirit is always present.

Suggested Reading: New Testament Conversions by Pastor George Gerberding

Benediction

Now unto him that is able to keep you from falling, and to present you faultless before the presence of his glory with exceeding joy, To the only wise God our Savior, be glory and majesty, dominion and power, both now and ever. Amen. (Jude 1:24-25)

More Than 100 Good Christian Books For You To Download And Enjoy

The Book of Concord. Edited by Henry Eyster Jacobs and Charles Krauth.

Henry Eyster Jacobs. *Summary of the Christian Faith*

Theodore Schmauk. *The Confessional Principle and The Confessions of The Lutheran Church As Embodying The Evangelical Confession of The Christian Church*

George Gerberding. *Life and Letters of William Passavant*

Joseph Stump. *Life of Philip Melanchthon*

John Morris. *Life Reminiscences of An Old Lutheran Minister*

Matthias Loy. *The Doctrine of Justification*

Matthias Loy. *The Story of My Life*

William Dau. *Luther Examined and Reexamined*

Simon Peter Long. *The Great Gospel*

George Schodde *et al*. *Walther and the Predestination Controversy. The Error of Modern Missouri*

John Sander. *Devotional Readings from Luther's Works*

A full catalog of all 100+ downloadable titles is available at LutheranLibrary.org .

Made in the USA
Las Vegas, NV
16 September 2021